TAKE YE EAT

"Man shall not live by bread alone, but by every word that proceedeth out of the mouth of God"

Matthew 4:4

LENA M. WILLIAMS MCMILLON

Presented to

_____

From

_____

Date

_____

Occasion

_____

INTRODUCTION

God wants you to be healthy, happy and secure in His love. He wants you to prosper and enjoy abundant living here and now Therefore He has given to you specific instructions regarding how to attain all that you desire. The Holy Bible is our instruction book. It contains the age old secrets of the way to successful living - few there be that find it.

In the midst of the garden of paradise is the tree of wisdom. Her fruits are riches, honor, and length of days. Adam and Eve ate from the tree of knowledge of good and evil, and brought forth all the problems that today exist. The tree of life was also in the midst of the garden.

"She is a tree of life...happy is everyone that lays hold on her, and happy is everyone that retaineth her" (Proverbs 3: 16-18). You can have love, happiness, good health, wealth, power and prosperity. You can be successful in all that you undertake to do, according to His word.

"For ye know the grace of our Lord Jesus Christ, that though he was rich, yet for your sakes he became poor, that ye through his poverty might be rich."

2 Cor. 8:9

CONTENTS

*"And he shewed me a pure river of water
of life, clear as crystal, proceeding out
of the throne of God and of the lamb.
In the midst of the street of it, and on
either side of the river, was there the
tree of life, which bare twelve manner of
fruit every month: and the leaves of the
tree were for the healing of the nations."*

Revelations 22: 1-2

WISDOM: A TREE OF LIFE

We are first introduced to the tree of life in Genesis 2:9 *"And out of the ground made the Lord God to grow every tree that is pleasant to the sight, and good for food; the tree of life also in the midst of the garden, and the tree of knowledge of good and evil."*

Proverbs 3: 13-19 identifies the tree and fruits of it, and also describes the results of partaking of her fruits.

Note: *"Happy is the man that findeth* **wisdom**.....*She is a tree of life to them that retaineth her.....*****Length of days*** *is in her right hand; and in her left hand* **riches and honor***. The Lord by wisdom hath founded the earth."*

Revelation 2:7 makes it known to us that this tree of life is still available to us! *"He that hath an ear, let him hear what the Spirit saith unto the churches: To him that overcometh will I give to eat of the tree of life, which is in the midst of the paradise of God. "*This may be paraphrased to read *"Anyone that can understand the principles of divine love and truth and apply the teaching and doctrines of the Holy Scriptures, wisdom will enable him to overcome the problems of the world and live a rich, honorable and abundant life."*

Our Lord was hung on a cross between two thieves. One of them mocked him while the other said unto him, "Remember me when thou come unto thy kingdom." This thief, unlike the other malefactor, recognizing his own poor state of being, spoke with wisdom. He was seeking deliverance from his own predicament rather than mocking another. Jesus' response was, "Verily I say unto thee, today shalt thou be with me in paradise."

These two men can be seen to represent the attitude of all mankind. We may elect to either mock the Christ, while the good call upon Him to enter into the paradise of God, or we can mock this very teaching and continue on in our own unprofitable way. It is because of the foolishness of mankind's disregard for the divine Laws of God that brings discord into our lives. When we learn the significance of God's divine Laws to our well-being we will begin to enter into paradise. Jesus did not tell this man to wait until the "hereafter" or even until tomorrow, but he promised him that he would be with him in paradise that same day. God has not told us that we have to wait for blessings in the hereafter "over yonder-somewhere in the sky bye and bye." It may be this false concept that prevents many from trusting in God's Word. But we must first realize that God's laws are love, truth, light, and wisdom. They are for now and forevermore bringing about the ultimate good in the lives of men.

Mankind's expulsion from the garden of Eden, and his loss of access to the tree of life can readily be understood if we first consider the two trees mentioned, both in the midst of the garden. The tree of knowledge of good and evil represents humanity's natural perception of the world around him. Mankind's logic and man's reasoning. Mankind's rationale is a combination of good and evil, for his seeing and hearing is imperfect. There are many things the natural eye cannot see, there are many things the natural ear cannot hear.

The tree of life represents the wisdom of God.

"God saw everything that he had made, and, behold it was very good" (Genesis 1:31). If man had eaten of the tree of life, he would have been able to behold the good and would never have experienced shame, doubts, or fear. Man chose to eat of the tree of knowledge.

Commit Roman 8:28 to memory; *"And we know that all things work together for good to them that love God, to them who are called according to his purpose."* This includes you! When would-be assailants, circumstances, adverse conditions and enemies arise, apply this verse. Wisdom declares, knowing that all things work to bring about your good, *"Though you meant it for evil, God meant it for good."*

You must do more than say this, you must believe it. According to your belief so be it unto you. Know there is power beyond that you can see, hear or know - powers that create, regulate, and establish whatever you, through faith, can believe. This is wisdom. Take ye, eat.

The hymn writer has said;

"When waves of affliction sweep over the soul, and sunlight is *hidden from view, if ever you're tempted to fret or complain, just think of his goodness to you.*

The world may forsake you, and those whom you trust may prove to be false and untrue, there's one you can trust even to the end, just think of his goodness to you.

. . . . Just think of his goodness to you, yes, think of his goodness to you; Tho storms o'er thee sweep, he is *able to keep, O think of his goodness to you."*

"Wisdom hath builded her house, she hath hewn out her seven pillars; She hath killed her beasts; She hath mixed her wine; She hath furnished her table.........Whoso is *simple, let him turn in hither; as for him that lacketh understanding, she saith to him, come, eat of my bread, and drink of the wine which I have mixed"* (Proverbs 9:1-5).

Take ye, eat.

The Sermon on the Mount
Principles and Rules of the Kingdom:
The Beatitudes – perfect happiness or perfect blessedness.
Matthew 5:1-12 and Luke 6: 20-49

BEATITUDE: WHAT YOUR ATTITUDE SHOULD BE

Attitude is defined as:

1. the posture or position of a person showing or meant to show a mental state, emotion, or mood.

2. the manner of acting, feeling, or thinking that shows one's disposition, opinion, etc.

3. one's disposition, opinion, etc.

Be-attitude is the attitude we should hold toward others, nature, God, and the universe, that Jesus declared would bring happiness into our lives (Matthew 5:1-12).

The Sermon on The Mount delivered by the master teacher clearly outlines the attitudes we need for ultimate happiness: self-control, soberness, seeking for truth, kindness, understanding, honesty, loyalty, and pleasantness.

The word blessed has been used interchangeably with happy by many writers. I suggest that blessed has a much more profound connotation. Happy or blessed as used in this passage addresses more than the issue of one's feelings or emotions; it addresses itself to the totality of one's existence, now and forevermore. It addresses itself to mankind's ultimate happiness, farther than human eyes can see, or ears can hear, beyond human comprehension.

God wants the very best for you. He wants you to be happy, prosperous, in good health, and at peace with the universe. Many have harbored the erroneous belief that God wants man to suffer sickness, disease, and poverty........We often hear great sweltering testimonies of sorrow and despair in serving God and living "right," but little about the victories. By some stretch of these religious imaginations, this is seen somehow to be done to the glory of God!

You are invited to feast on the good news that Jesus proclaims in his sermon on the mount. As you consider these principles or attitudes, your spiritual digestive tract will begin to adjust not only to the milk of the word, which is salvation, but meat also, which is wisdom and understanding.

"Blessed are the poor in spirit, for theirs is the kingdom of heaven." Mankind is a part of the eternal purpose of God - whom he regenerates, sanctifies and saves in consistency with the free agency of man. Wisdom comprehends all the means of life in connection with the end, and it is a most glorious display of God's goodness; infinitely free and unchangeable. It excludes boasting and promotes humility and sober-mindedness.

*"Blessed are they that mourn for they shall be comforted. "*This can be seen as man's attitude toward man. It is a simple law of the harvest, whatsoever a man soweth that shall he also reap. If you show compassion to others, compassion will be shown to you. *"Being happy-go-lucky around a person whose heart is heavy is as bad as stealing his jacket in cold weather, or rubbing salt in his wounds"* (Proverbs 25:20).

"Blessed are the meek for they shall inherit the earth." How do you handle yourself? Meekness is having the ability to exercise self-control. To subdue yourself.

"A wise man controls his temper. He knows that anger causes great loss" (Proverbs 14:29). Meekness is not, as many have supposed, suffering in silence, but it is a master plan for success!

"Blessed are they who do hunger and thirst after righteousness; for they shall be filled." It seems as though in our religious vanity we have thought of the righteousness of God to be limited to our morality. While indeed our morals should be in accord with those principles set forth in the commandments, it is much more. It is the bringing forth of the right results according to God's eternal laws. Jesus is our righteousness, he makes things right with God for us. God has declared it so. Accept him.

"Blessed are the merciful; for they shall obtain mercy." We pray that God forgive us our debts as we forgive our debtors. If we forgive not others our heavenly Father will not forgive us. This is justice. This will bring about peace and harmony between God and mankind, for we can receive forgiveness from God only as we show mercy and forgive our fellowman.

"Blessed are the pure in heart for they shall see God. "It is out of the heart that flows the issues of life. Those with pure hearts will see the good in others, they will do good unto others, reject gossip, hatred, suspicion, and every evil and negative thought. If your heart is pure you will see God's handiwork in all creation.

"Blessed are the peacemakers for they shall be called the children of God. "It is obvious that greater happiness will be derived through keeping peace with others. This eliminates gossiping and meddling in the affairs of others. *"Fools start fights everywhere while wise men try to keep peace"* (Proverbs 29:8). To be a peacemaker, we must not only live

peaceably with our fellowman, but we must be in harmony with the laws of the universe, the land, the waters, arid all living creation.

"Blessed are they which are persecuted for righteousness sake; for theirs is the kingdom of God." Persecution is defined as oppressive treatment because of religion or beliefs. It is also defined as harassment. Righteousness encompasses all the truths of God's universe. God's laws regulate not only the morals of humanity but the mores of creation. Noah knew the taunts of harassers when he was building the Ark. Jesus Christ himself was persecuted. Early philosophers were subjected to religious harassment and oppression because of their declaration that the earth was round. Leonardo Da Vinci's idea of a horseless carriage met with ridicule. Orville and Wilbur Wright were ridiculed for their attempt to fly. If you seek for truth, "right ideas," contrary to popular belief you will suffer persecution, for so suffered the prophets before you. But success awaits those that are willing to press forward. Happiness is the reward of those who will dare seek the truths of the universe, knowing that these truths are of the kingdom of God.

"Blessed are ye when men revile you, persecute you, and shall say all manner of evil against you falsely, for my sake, rejoice and be exceedingly glad, for great is your reward in heaven: for so persecuted they the prophets before you." The greatest persecution suffered by man, is that persecution from man, inflicted upon man, because of man's relationship with man's God or gods.

Because of religious idiosyncrasies, the Israelites suffered persecution, the prophets suffered persecution, Christians suffered persecution. The Lord suffered the greatest persecution of all. He was reviled, all manner of evil was spoken against him, he was hung out on Calvary's cross, but on the third day he was raised up, declaring all power of heaven and earth was in his hand. He has shared this power and authority with the believers. They have been made joint-heirs to all the Father has given. All power in heaven and earth is yours if you are in

Christ and he is in you. If you trust him and have faith there is nothing impossible. All things are possible if you only believe.

"What things soever you desire, when you pray, believe that you receive them, and you shall have them" (Mark 11:24). Hallelujah and Amen!

IF YOU WOULD

If you would happy, live by the laws of the Lord,
If you would be prosperous, be governed by his word,
If you would find peace, promote universal harmony
If you would find truth, seek for it diligently.

If you would find mercy of God, show mercy unto others,
If you would be kept, keep peace with your brothers,
If you would walk with God, be true to yourself
If you would find good, strive not for fame nor pelf.

PRAYER: THE KEY
TO THE KINGDOM

One may ask, 'What is prayer?'

It has often been said that prayer is the key to the kingdom. A more formal definition of prayer is: A reverent petition made to deity or other objects of worship: A specially worded or spontaneously expressed appeal to God.

Many have viewed prayer as being mere ritualistic, religious verbalizations directed toward a god of people's imagination in the hope that He would be pleased and therefore grant them favors. It seems the unshakable faith of many that God doesn't always answer prayers, which makes their prayers at the most-expressed hope and perhaps only wishful thinking. The atheist views prayer as a crutch for the weak and the foolish. Most Christians agree that prayer is the spoken or unspoken sincere desires of the heart being made known to a true and living God.

Each of these definitions are true in part, at least to some, but neither are complete or altogether accurate. The full meaning of prayer is - that continual communion between God and creation which produces the ultimate good. Although we, being finite beings, may not perceive all as being good Scriptures teaches that God beheld all that he had made and said it was very good.

Often we hear these words in religious assemblies "Shall we Pray?" How do we pray? It would be according to which group we were associated with. From the very beginning man has used many methods or forms of ritualistic behavior in his effort to control circumstances or conditions around him. He has used magic incantations in various rites, to have ample supplies of food, to overcome enemies, to produce rain, to bless, to curse, to bury their dead, and to reproduce. He has fasted, he has abstained from sex, he has anointed himself with oils, he has cried with loud wailings, he has rent his clothing, distorted his face, moaned sorrowfully, he has sprinkled blood, he has sprinkled water, he has immersed himself in consecrated waters and all these things he has done in various positions: Kneeling, squatting, lying prostrate, sitting, often with limbs wrapped around limb like a pretzel, Hands folded, hands lifted, hands joined, hands wringing, hands flailing or even clapping. As every person must live and communicate with others on his level, in the language he understands, so must every person commune with God. The time, place, or circumstances are relevant only to he who worships. We do not need to criticize others, for as members of various religious groups we adopt certain practices. Our geographical environment as well as our ethnic origin dictates our religious affiliations and practices to a large degree.

"God is a Spirit; and they that worship him must worship him in *spirit and* in *truth"(John* 4:24). On the conscious level we are often limited by circumstances; however, there is another level that some refer to as the subconscious level. A more accurate expression is the spiritual level. We, being yet in the flesh, are also spirit beings, the express image of a Spirit Being, with all the physical aspects and peculiarities of our person serving as escalators to elevate us to higher heights or lower depths. Mankind is the image of God.

Although man is like God, God is not like man. As we gaze into a mirror our image reflected is like us but we are not like a mirror. For as we gaze before a mirror, an image of our being is reflected, having no power to move or exist aside from us. So it is with God and man. Luke

18 suggests that man must always pray and not faint, not to boast but to be honest with himself and with God. **Not** *faint* **means not to give up, but to persevere, don't lose heart, to be steadfast in purpose.**

THE PRAYER OF FAITH

There are many forms of prayer, but the prayer of faith is the prayer you believe, nothing more and certainly nothing less. It will not do you any good to say you believe something if you do not. Religious rites or ceremony cannot change this fact. The prayer you believe is the prayer that is answered (Matthew 21:22).

What is it that we believe? Environment plays its part as does our ethnic background. Those things which we believe are those things which we have been taught, either by precept or example. If you were born and lived in China you would probably be inclined to adhere to Buddhism or Hinduism. If you were born in Africa your praise would probably be to the beat of the drum and the dance. If you were born of the Jew you would probably keep the Passover, Purim and Hanukah. If you are the offspring of Christian parents you will probably believe in Christianity. Of course, humanity as free agents can and do sometimes change, but even change will be a result of exposure to other ways or thoughts.

Whatever man comes to believe, whatever the folklore, the language, or religion or absence of it, humans will commune with God. Man will be recipient of God's benefits whether he acknowledges it or not. For the sun shines on the just and unjust (Matthew 5:45). Also Scripture teaches that *"every knee must bow and every tongue confess that Jesus Christ is Lord"(Phil.* 2:11). Man is subject to his power with or without man's consent! However there is another dimension; as a free agent man may believe anything he so chooses. God promises that *"all things, whatever ye ask in prayer, believing, ye shall receive"* (Matthew 21:22).

Prayer is the key to the kingdom – your faith unlocks the door!

Prayer of Submission

There is the prayer of submission. Isaiah prayed, "Here am I Lord, send me." Jesus prayed, "Nevertheless not my will but thine be done." The Virgin Mary affirmed, "Behold, I am the handmaid of the Lord; be it unto me according to your word." With these spoken words was the spirit of submission. Prayer to be effective must be more than spoken words, it must be a continual communion with God.

The divine will of God is for the ultimate good of all creation and you will be a part of this will with or without your consent. God's ways are unchangeable, they are everlasting. Submission to the Almighty will bring great rewards and alleviate much suffering. Nature itself must submit to the Almighty in giving, yielding her fruits to all that will ask of her. *"God resisteth the proud, but giveth grace unto the humble. Submit yourselves, therefore to God"* (James 4:7). *"Obey them that have rule over you, and submit yourselves; for they watch for your souls, as they that must give account, that they may do it with joy, and not with grief; for that is unprofitable to you"* (Hebrew 13: 17). This reference is to your spiritual leaders. Many hardships are suffered because of arrogance toward spiritual leaders.

There is a way of things. God's way is not like man's. God has a divine plan for man but man must follow the plan for his ultimate success. Submissiveness is to learn God's way, follow the way, walk in the way, and believe in the way, then everything for you will go the right way! Your very submissiveness becomes your victory. When we learn why the wind blows we will discover that it blows for us. Let the wind blow as it will and it will take you where you will, but don't set your sail against the wind---for then you will be hurled down by the supreme will—a mass of submissiveness with a broken will. *"It is hard to kick against the pricks"* (Acts 9).

PRAYER OF INTERCESSION

There is the prayer of intercession. It recognizes that the natural laws of nature were set in motion by the God of creation. It was God who established the law of the harvest; "that whatsoever man soweth that shall he also reap." It was God who made two great lights and the stars also; the greater to rule the day and the lesser to rule the night. It was God who so decreed that the waters be gathered unto one place that dry land would appear. It was God who established the law that the earth bring forth the herb, yielding seed after its kind: and the fruit tree, yielding seed after its kind. It is God's law that declares that the soul that sinneth will surely die. All these are laws He in His infinite wisdom established to govern His universe by the powers that be. There is a greater power, his prayer power. Because of the prayers of the righteous, God has so elected to intervene in sundry times and in divers manners in the natural working of His universe.

It was by this power Joshua commanded the sun to stand still at Gibeon and the moon in the Valley of Aijalon. It was by this power that Moses parted the Red Sea and permitted the Israelites to cross over on dry land. It was by this power that the dead have been raised. It was by this power that the law of sin no longer has power over those declared righteous by God. It was by this power demons were cast out, blind were made to see, the lame made to walk and the dumb made to talk. Intercessory prayer is simply praying in someone else's behalf. Jesus prayed an intercessory prayer before he went to Calvary. He prayed *"Father, I will that they also, whom thou has given me, be with me where I am, that they may behold my glory, which thou hast given me; for thou lovedst me before the foundation of the world"* (John 17:24). John 17 is the Lord's intercessory prayer for believers. He prayed that those kept in his name would have the right to intercede, for he has bestowed his glory upon all that believe.

THE PRAYER OF PRAISE AND THANKSGIVING

"Let everything that has breath praise the Lord, praise ye the Lord."

The prayer of praise is the highest form of communion with God. It is taking delight in the law of the Lord, the beauty and magnificence of all creation. "Delight yourself in the law of the Lord and he will give you the desires of your heart." Declare as the Psalmist, "Bless the Lord O my soul and all that is within me, bless his holy name. Bless the Lord O my soul and forget not all his benefits, who gives generously all things." True praise is to thank him because he is so good, thank him for his lovingkindness, thank him for his mighty miracles, praise him for the heavens and for the heavenly lights, for the moon and stars at night. True praise is to find joy in the soft sweet fragrance of flowers, the cool liquid greenness of the grass, the ripplings of flowing rivers, the awesomeness of raging waters, the peace and tranquility of still waters. To praise God is to know joy beyond laughter or tears, beyond sorrow or fears; to know joy beyond your sight, and find security in his might.

"Make a joyful noise unto the LORD, all ye lands. Serve the LORD with gladness: Come before His presence with singing. Know ye that the LORD He is God: It is He that hath made us and not we ourselves: We are His people, and the sheep of His pasture. Enter into His gates with thanksgiving and into His courts with praise; be thankful unto Him and bless His name. For the LORD is good; His mercy is everlasting. And His truth endureth to all generations" (Psalm 100).

FAITH:
UNLOCKS THE DOOR

Faith is a powerful, unseen spiritual force that enables anyone who applies faith to be what they want to be, do what they want to do and to have what they want to have. Jesus spoke to the Syrophenician woman (and to all who will believe) *"Great is thy faith, be it unto you as thou will"* (Matthew 15:28). Social protocol, cultural traditions or religious mores have no power over the working of your faith. Jesus had reminded this woman that it was not right, according to tradition, to give the children's bread to "dogs." He was not calling this woman a dog but those that were not Jews or believers were referred to as dogs, (meaning outside of the household) Anyone not a Jew was outside the household of faith. This Syrophenician woman understood the terminology of her day as reflected in her response: "Truth, Lord; yet even (pets) dogs eat the crumbs which fall from their master's table." For pets are allowed inside the house! Jesus was not trying to insult this woman! He was conversing with her on a level with which she was familiar. He proceeded to let her know that she had all that was needed to get what she wanted, (she had the power of faith). It was because of her faith, not because of her race, sex, or religion, that he spoke to her, saying "Woman, great is thy faith, be it unto you even as thou will." He responds at the level of your faith.

If you have faith, you have the right and you have the might to be what you want to be, have what you want to have, and do what you want to do. Often we hear the statement, "I don't have the faith!" Everyone has faith. Everything we do is an act of faith, either in someone or something. When we get behind the wheel of our car, turn on the ignition, set it in drive, put our foot on the accelerator, we're acting on faith—faith that this machine will move and take us where we steer it to go. When we report to our places of employment, perform various tasks for a specified period of time, we have faith that a paycheck is forthcoming. When we purchase a ticket and climb aboard one of those big jet airliners, strap ourselves into our seat, this is an act of faith. We don't understand all the particulars of the plane, nor do we necessarily know the pilot, but we expect to reach our destinations. However, it seems that we have difficulty in exercising faith in an Almighty God, the creator of the heavens and earth.

What is faith? *"Faith is the substance of things hoped for, the evidence of things not seen. By it the elders received a good report. Through faith we understand that the worlds were framed by the word of God, so that things which are seen were not made of things which do appear"* (Hebrew 11: 1-3). For example, a tomato seed is very small, it is the seed of a tomato, but is itself not a tomato. However all the substance of the tomato is contained within the seed. A tomato seed will not produce a tomato unless it is planted, watered and receives light! Faith can be seen as a seed, but it must be a seed of hope, sprinkled with prayers according to the light of the word!

What can you do with faith? Jesus taught his disciples saying, *"if ye have faith and doubt not, ye shall say unto this mountain, be thou removed and cast into the sea, and it shall be done...and all things, whatsoever ye shall ask in prayer, believing, ye shall receive"* (Matthew 21).

The Bible tells us that "by faith Sarah received strength to conceive after she had passed child-bearing age; by faith Moses' parents hid him in the bulrushes that he may not be killed by Pharaoh; by faith Rahab the harlot was saved and did not perish with them that did not believe;

by faith women received their loved ones back from the dead, they were raised to life again."

Faith is a powerful force given to us, it is a gift from God. By your faith you can have what you want to have, be what you want to be, do what you want to do. But if you do not use your faith you will lose it.

"Faith cometh by hearing (understanding) and hearing by the word of God"(Roman 10:17). When you **know** better, you'll do better. Unlock the door to all you can hope for, all the Kingdom of God is yours.

Too many Christians are hesitant to believe that God means exactly what He says. They seem to feel that it is incredible that He should entrust them with His infinite power. They lack spiritual understanding to comprehend the purpose of their Heavenly Father to bring the redeemed of the Lord into the true administration of His kingdom. But this is in fact the divine plan of God from the beginning. Carnal Christians think it strange that God in this present age wants His people to develop their spiritual powers, to be willing to unashamedly share in the ministry of redeeming, healing, and teaching with authority, now and through the coming age.

Christian believers do not have to fear accepting the authority given them. God wants His people to live victoriously, actively intervening on behalf of others and actively entering into His perfect plan of salvation for the body, mind, and spirit - the whole man - ministering to all man's needs. We have the assurance of God that our faith will be backed by His power. The Christian believer's faith is the power-line connected to the power-house to give light to the world.

God will grant your petitions according to your own heart, and will fulfil your counsel. It is all according to what you will believe in your heart. When you reach that degree of faith you will be partakers of all the Father's benefits, you will live an abundant life. The deep reality of the relationship between the Father and the redeemed of the

Lord is little comprehended by the great majority of believers. Jesus compared the relationship of the head (His relationship with believers) to the members of the body. Where there is good health, members are responsive to the slightest direction of the head. But if members are afflicted there will be a malfunctioning of the body. Some members of the body will be inaccurate in carrying out their functions. When faith is weak, there is a malfunctioning of the spiritual body of believers. Some members of the body are not able to function as they should, others are paralyzed and not functioning at all. The problem is often because they are malnourished. They have not fed their spiritual man with the true principles set forth in the word of God.

The spiritual body of Christ, which is the body of Christian believers, has this promise from the head: "If ye abide in me, and my words abide in you, you shall ask what ye will, and it shall be done unto you" (John 15: 7).

Notice that this promise is that it will be done unto you, not for you. The members of the body send out demands for the needs of the body. When members of the body are not "diseased" and are able to function as they should, they will respond to the direction of the head, but will not expect the head to perform the task! So it is with the spiritual body of Christ, when members are spiritually healthy, they will accept directions from the head and function accordingly.

Too often, Christians assume a passive attitude that accepts anything that comes to them as the will of God, contenting themselves with a submissive uttering of "Thy will be done." Jesus Christ, the head of the Christian body of believers, plainly instructs the believers that *"ye shall ask what ye will and it will be done unto you"* (John 15:17). Not to do so would be an act of disbelief, it would be to shirk not only a divine benefit but your earthly responsibility to function as a member of the body to the good of mankind. We are to positively will the will of the Father, seek out His revelations, and to function in assurance according to His word. Then our prayer, "thy will be done" will be spoken in power of the assurance: *"In this is my Father glorified, that ye bear much fruit; so shall ye be my disciples"* (John 15:8). Jesus is plainly stating that it is the will of the Father that we bear much fruit. Therefore He (the Father) is glorified that ye ask what ye will that it may be done unto you! Much of the weakness of the church is due to its failure to fully understand this all-important truth.

It is God's will that mankind comes to the place of exercising authority over the works of God as it was planned in the counsels of eternity (Psalm 8). In the closing chapter of Matthew we are shown the King of kings on a mountain in Galilee speaking to his followers, declaring: "All authority both in heaven and earth has been given unto me." It is a profound spiritual truth that the authority of the risen Christ at the right hand of the throne of the Majesty in the heavens, is to reach its full development and manifestation through the body of believers.

It is a great honor and responsibility for the Christian members set forth in Roman 8:17, that we are heirs of God and joint heirs with Christ, for we are risen with him. Total salvation in Christ involves more than remission for sins, but it is the gift of God to abundant, eternal life. Salvation covers sin, sickness, and scarcity! The church, which is the body of Christ, has a great responsibility. For the coming age of the body and its entrance upon the prepared inheritance, all the rest of God's creation is waiting with earnest expectation. Many obstacles confront the believer in his ministry. They block the way, they shut out the vision ahead, they will render the worker immobile if he fails to exercise his authority. There are many mountains that are in the pathway of fulfillment, these mountains are too varied in nature to particularize, but they are hindrances to the fulfillment of God's plan for us. Some pray for the Lord to remove their mountains, others pray for the mountains not to be removed, but that they be led around them. How do you pray, according to your fear or your faith? Fear says you may not want the mountain moved, faith trusts in the word. The word has specific instructions on how to deal with the mountains, yet we rationalize – "the mountain may be someone near and dear to us, unless we climb the mountain we'll never get to the other side, etc." We time and again choose to ignore or explain away the command of faith we have been given.

How soon we forget that we are told that we wrestle not against flesh and blood but spiritual powers. Jesus said in Matthew 21:22 *"if ye say unto this mountain, be thou removed, and be thou cast into the sea, it shall be done."* However this is followed by a promise contingent upon your faith. Commands are given by the believer in the name of Jesus. How often we attempt to reverse this divine order by commanding Christ to perform certain tasks at our request. How quick we are to claim our inability to function, denying what Christ said was possible for us to accomplish. Albeit it with great humility we make God a liar. We have been commissioned and given the authority to act in the name of Jesus according to the Word of God. We have the promise (John 16:23) *"Verily, verily, I say unto you, whatever ye shall ask the Father in my name, he will give it you. "*

We need to know that authority is not in prayer alone. Prayer is communication with God, not authority over God to direct him in what we think he ought to do. By our faith we have authority or power. We have authority to act in the name of Jesus. Moses was questioned by God: (Exodus 14:15) *"Wherefore criest thou unto me?"* (you) *"Speak unto the children of Israel that they go forward. ""Lift up thy rod and stretch out thine hand over the sea, and divide it."* Here Moses had been praying for the Lord to work for him, but God asked him, "Why are you asking me to do this for you, you lift up your rod, take action, and I will be with you. I will see that you are able to accomplish the task, but I'm not going to do it for you, I want you to do it."

Likewise when we have instruction from the Word of God, and when we will act on the word in faith, we have God's promise that he will back up whatever we do and that it will come to pass, as we will. God said to Moses and He is saying to you- "You have asked me to work; I have granted your request, but I choose to do the work through you; speak to the obstacle before you in my name, and it will obey."

The present age is one in which God endeavors to train representatives and ambassadors for a future and mightier work in cooperation with His Son, Believers represent a Volunteer Army, ready and willing to enter into battle. The responsibility for accepting or rejecting this offer lies with the individual believer. The Apostles warn us that *"we wrestle not against flesh and blood, but against the principalities, against the powers, against the world rulers of darkness, against the spiritual host of wickedness in the heavenlies"* (Ephesians 6:12). We must learn the secret of victory through authority, as well as through prayer, and then Christ's church will become a place of strength for the lost. We pray for strength, we pray with intensity that it be released in our midst. Are we fulfilling the condition? Are we providing the line of faith through which the power of God is released?

Those intercessors with the authority of the Most High, functioning by the power of God, are those believers, men and women, whose eyes are open to the full knowledge of their place in Christ.

To such, the Word of God is a battle chart on which is the detailed plan of action. Such men and women know that they are appointed by Him to act according to his word. Such as these will not be lifted up in pride or in their own self-righteousness but will be deeply conscious of their own unworthiness and inadequacy, but believe God's Word and be willing to act accordingly without fear of fault or failure. They will realize the heavenly responsibility which rests upon them and will be in tune with the will of God concerning the method of the advancement of His kingdom. The working of the body of Christ, the church, has been held back not for lack of human laborers or finances but because of lack of understanding. For lack of understanding God's people are destroyed (Hosea 4:6).

Understanding of the mighty mysteries of the heavenly comes only to those men and women who are able to receive them. It is not only the privilege but the responsibility of every Christian to fully understand the divine desire for the perfecting of our ministry and to claim their place in Christ.

There is no other method for the Christian to function with the power invested in him except by an unwavering belief that God will perform every work he has promised. There are no fleshly works of self-denial, no self-righteousness, not even the morals of the most upright that we can depend on, but it is by faith in God. By faith we realize that the Lord himself is the strength of our countenance, as his power works through us in our ministry. Having this assurance, the Christian believer is able to confront whatever situations that may arise, calmly and fearlessly, knowing that "if the Lord be for us who can be against us?" When this attitude is maintained without doubt, a change will come, and the attacks will lose their force. Victory belongs to the children of God. We have been made Kings and Priests unto God. If we believe this and walk in the consciousness of the Lord, inspired and energized with a new vision of the coming kingdom, the body of Christ will rise in the name of the Lord and with the authority given unto us and refuse to be subject to any interference with its mission. Attacks on physical health, attacks on family and social relationships, attacks on financial matters, attacks on the mental faculties are all to be put under subjection by the authority of the Most High God according to His word! These are matters that frequently block the program of Christ's church, but they too shall fall before the intercessor when we speak in the name of Jesus, nothing doubting. Perhaps the hardest lesson that must be learned by every Christian seeking after the deeper life of Christ, is to be aware that each new appropriation of grace and knowledge will bring them into more subtle conflict. With further advancement in the knowledge of the Lord, there comes a startling realization that the very heavenly places are also habitats of the power of darkness. Christians must know that our seat with Christ places us "far above all principalities, powers, and might, and dominion" and that we are provided with authority and power for victory so long as we maintain our place. There must be no double-mindedness.

It is common to hear Christians attribute every national calamity as being "an act of God", when such should be laid at the door of that restless and relentless enemy of mankind, called Satan. Of course it is true that the permission of the Most High has been given, but there is among the majority of God's people an inability to discern in their own suffering what is the chastening of the Lord or what is due to the oppression of the enemy.

Consequently too many Christians are being beaten down to the ground, unable to rise again. They're stricken with poor health, poverty, family problems, religious problems, paranoia of fellow Christians, burdened down with the cares of this world and deceived into believing it is their lot in life—into believing that it is because of their Christianity that it is so. Those walking in the authority of God's Word must appreciate the reality of this danger, and teach the body of Christ the truth of the word "ye shall know the truth and the truth shall make you free."

The truth and life is Jesus, the Christ. He said, *"I am come that they may have life and have it more abundantly"* (John 10:10).

Let us not dishonor the Word of God by believing that God will receive any glory from one of His children enduring such hardship. As it was with Moses at the Red Sea, so it yet is with every consecrated hand that lifts the rod of authority against unseen powers of darkness. Your rod of authority is your faith. Your faith can overcome every obstacle.

Take ye, eat.

HEALTH: YOUR BODY, MIND, AND SPIRIT

It is now being acknowledged by physicians that disease is not so much in the body as it is first in the mind, for it is in the mind that disease or healing first occurs. Ancient Egyptians and Brahmans understood that concentrating their attention on the power of their conscious mind would overcome physical conditions. Life is a form of energy that must be guarded and directed within the human body, mind and spirit.

The mind is the most colossal power of this world, for the mind is the God-part of mankind. The power of the mind has been neglected far too long by physiologists and economists and hardly even noticed by physicians. The mind is a source of power which we habitually fail to use or worse--we habitually choose to misuse. Most people do not seem to be aware of this colossal power of the mind, which has enough energy to destroy a city. The great physician and master teacher, Jesus, pointed out the source of man's unlimited power when he said *"The Kingdom of God is within you"(Luke* 17:31). Psychologists are now beginning to recognize the wisdom of Paul's teaching to the Romans: *"Be ye transformed by the renewing of your* mind" (Romans 12:2). They are beginning to realize that the mind can produce changes in the external. Although mind power has been used by mankind throughout the ages, it is time Christians begin to use it deliberately and constructively to overcome the world, increase their wealth and improve their health.

Faith is a dynamic power of the mind. Healing power is stored in the body, which is released through words of faith. When faith is released by the spoken word, a chemical change takes place in the body. Your spoken words of faith have life-giving, healing power. This truth was emphasized by Jesus when he promised, *"Verily I say unto you, whosoever shall say unto this mountain be thou removed and cast into the sea; and shall not doubt in his heart, but believe that what he saith comes to pass; he shall have it. Therefore I say unto you, all things whatsoever ye ask for, believe that ye receive them, and ye shall have them"* (Mark 11:22-24).

By the mind power of faith within, electronic energies of brain electrons are released. This process hastens the process of nature and healing results are quickly produced that would have taken much longer or would not have occurred at all. The mind has the power to cause disease in the body and the power to overcome it. The mind operates according to beliefs. However, one thing that needs to be realized is this: thoughts and ideas are not necessarily beliefs. Jesus said *"all things are possible to him that believeth"(Mark* 9:23). When his disciples inquired on one occasion why they had not been able to heal in some cases - Jesus replied, *"because of your unbelief"* (Matthew 17:20). They undoubtedly had the thoughts and ideas about healing, but they were without belief.

Faith works to bring about success or failure, sickness or disease, poverty or riches. According to your faith it will be done unto you. This is a spiritual teaching found throughout the Scriptures. Whatever you are totally convinced about, that you have unbending faith in, that you have no doubt about is that which you have faith in.

Whatever you expect is that which you have faith in. Whatever you prepare for is that which you have faith in. These things will be made manifest in your life. You can build faith or strengthen your faith. You do not have to be one of "little faith" or one of "little power." Faith is a result of certain processes of the body, mind, and spirit working in unity. *"Faith cometh by hearing, (body function) and hearing (under-standing of the mind) by the word of God"* (spiritual part) (Romans 10: 17). Hearing with the ears is the physical part. Hearing in the next usage is referring to your understanding, or the mental part, and the Word of God is spirit. Faith that is built on the Word of God will produce only good in your life.

There is a faith produced by negative ideas, negative things we hear and choose to believe. This faith will produce negative results: poverty, lack, sickness, diseases, discontentment, distrust, and all kinds of unhappiness. Yet there are those that will defend this belief to the end. They will insist that it is God's will for such to be. Those who do not attribute it to God's will declare that it is only natural and should be expected. Faith is the perception of the mind which will cause your belief to be made manifest. Faith is a power you are using all of the time, to produce either good or evil. If you want your faith to produce good in your life, to keep you in good health, and good spirit, keep your mind on the good things. Paul said (Phil 4:8) *"Whatsoever things are true, whatsoever things are honest, whatsoever things are just, whatso-ever things are pure, whatsoever things are lovely, whatsoever things are of good report, if there be any other virtue, and if there be any praise, think on these things."* How much plainer can this precept be made? Think good thoughts, think about lovely things of life, think of that which is admirable, think success, talk success, praise God for all things you desire and they will become a part of your life. You will have what you think you can, do what you think you can do and be what you think you can be. *"As a man thinketh, so is he"*(Proverbs 23:7).

By speaking positive words of power you can create and strengthen your faith, thus increasing the well-being of all your concerns. In de-veloping your faith, dwell upon the promises of God that proclaim the power of faith such as; *"thy faith hath made thee whole," "according to your faith so be* it *unto you,' "all things are possible if you believe."* Confess as Samuel did (II Sam 22:33) *"God is my strength and my power, and He maketh my way perfect.* "Confess good in your own words, from your heart! Speak words such as these aloud to yourself (look into a mirror, and bless yourself) "all things work for my good," "Strength and power are mine," "good things come my way," "health is mine," "I am healthy," "wealth is mine," "I am wealthy," "Love is mine," "I am loved and I am loving," "Happiness is mine," "I cast all evil from my life," "I am a blessing to others," "I am a child of God." As you speak words over and over such as these, you will feel a quickening in your body, a renewal of your mind, and an awakening of your spiritual powers. Do not expect instantaneous change, it takes time to develop your faith. As you continue to develop spiritually and mentally by affirming good, by "blessing yourself," good will begin to come to you. Remember you must not be selfish, but you must "also bless others." As you continue to confess and affirm good with the words of your mouth and meditation of your heart, you can confidently expect good to come to you.

You will begin to feel good because you have awakened your entire being to expect God's good for your body, mind, and spirit.

Speak only good for others and only good of others; be careful to let no evil communication come from your mouth, or from your heart, or from your mind. It costs you too much! Whatsoever you send out will return to you, increased! You must be careful to guard your heart and mind with all diligence. Do not remain in the company of those speaking negatively; do not be drawn into their gossip. Do not be a willing listener to foolishness. Avoid aggressive, hostile people, they are trouble-makers. Seek the company of the wise, those persons who strive for high ·ideals. Guard against jealousy, envy, hate, and all evil thoughts. These are forces that cause many of the body's diseases. Misuse of the mind power plays havoc on your health. It has long been known that stress, anxiety, worry and such produce stomach problems, indigestion, and ulcers. It is being recognized more and more that many of the body's illnesses are a result of the mind. Evil thoughts strip away youth, leave their ugly imprint on the faces of their owners.

There is a growing number of professionals who proclaim that throat problems such as goiters, tonsillitis, thyroid disturbances and other irritations are commonly seen in complainers, criticizers, gossips, evil communicators and those quick to express anger. Strong thoughts in the mind bring about a change in body chemistry. Hate may understandably be a cause of cancer and tumors. Hate which continues and is uncontrolled is deadly! Bitterness, jealousy, envy and rage lead to arthritis and rheumatism and if not checked it can lead to paralysis. Jealousy and envy that is internalized will produce skin rashes and skin diseases. There is an old saying that says someone is "green with envy." This is more than just a saying, for it has been noted by doctors that the skin does indeed turn green with envy, just as it will turn pink when blushing. However blushing is healthy. Heart disease is common among the suspicious minded, those who have a fear of others, and see people as being malicious and "cold-hearted." Impatience and intolerance of others often produce problems in the region of the back and neck. It reflects their "unbending stiff-necked" attitude. Headaches are most common with the high-tempered and those quick to speak their mind, blow-off steam or "blow their top." Eye and ear trouble is indicative of stubbornness, not being able to see another's point of view or to listen to another's point of view. Problems of the lower extremities, feet and ankles can be attributed to the immoral—feet that carry you swiftly into mischief. Whenever you fail to live according to the principles you know to be best, problems will usually result.

If you want to be in good health, body, mind and spirit, you must be careful and choose wisely those things you think, say or do. People who constantly talk of disease and worry over them invariably attract disease to themselves. To produce the very best in your life, constantly speak words of vitality, health, prosperity and praise. The body's forces will be transformed by the power of the mind, and transform your world into what you desire it to be. *Be not conformed to the world, but be ye transformed by the renewing of your mind*" (Romans 12:2). Your mind is renewed by positive thoughts.

TAKE YE EAT

Take ye eat and live
Whatsoever thou wouldest receive, give.
Forsake ye the ways of strife
Take ye eat from the tree of life.
Her fruits are riches, honor and length of days
Peace and pleasantness are her ways,
Bringing forth abundant joy and happiness,
Take ye, eat and be blest.

PROSPERITY: TITHES, FORESIGHT AND OBEDIENCE

Abraham learned the prosperity principle of tithing, Jacob used it when he left home to seek his fortune in a new land. Moses emphasized this prosperity principle among his people. It was practiced by the Israelites. The ancients knew the wisdom of giving. They understood it to be a universal principle. Giving in order to receive is the law of the harvest. You must give to receive exhale to inhale, sow to reap, give forgiveness to receive forgiveness. You can expect to receive in return for the substance you have given – multiplied – whatever that substance may be. *"Be not deceived, God is not mocked, Whatever a man soweth, that shall he also* reap"(Galatians 6:7). *"Give and it shall be given unto you, pressed down, shaken together and running over"* (Luke 6:38). This principle of God's universal law works whether you want it to or not. It works whether you believe it or not. It works whether you like it or not. If you do not give voluntarily, you will be made to give by force and generally under unhappy or unpleasant circumstances. If you fail to give of yourself, and of your resources, you can expect sickness, financial problems, problems in your relationships and affairs. When you give your financial affairs will improve as well as other areas of your life.

Giving of your finances is stressed because your finances represent your time, labor, needs, desires and almost everything that concerns the material world. Unfortunately, many Christians have rejected this principle, declaring they have no concern for the things of the world. Churches, because of this erroneous attitude, find themselves unable to function as they should in meeting some of the material needs of her people. Her member's needs continue to increase and the Church resources decrease while those of the world continue to generously support its pleasures and desires. Without question, millions of dollars are invested daily in games, entertainment, debauchery, and moral decadence. Consequently moral decadence and debauchery continue to increase and overflow within our society and make rich its investors. The world is using the law of giving and receiving, while our church members debate over whether tithing is for the New Testament Church or just for the Israelites. In the meantime we continue with our rituals of worship and money channeled into other areas. Jesus said, *"Where your treasure is, there will your heart be also"* (Matthew 6:21).

Tithing was first mentioned in Genesis 14:20, when Abraham gave his tithe to the High Priest of Salem. It was believed by the ancients that ten percent of the tithe was the number for increase. They believed and practiced regularly giving a tenth of all their income – the first portion to the Lord. Abraham received the promise *"Fear not, I am thy shield, and thy exceeding great reward"* (Genesis 15: l). Abraham was rich. Consistent, regular tithing, giving a tenth of your income to the church or spiritual organization to which you belong is a sure way to prosperity. "Prove me herewith, saith the Lord of hosts, if I will not open you the windows of heaven, and pour you out a blessing, that there shall not be room enough to receive it." He further promised to *"rebuke the devourer for your sake, and he shall not destroy the fruits of your ground; neither shall your vine cast her fruit before the time in the field, saith the Lord of hosts."*(Malachi 3: 10-11).

You have a promise here that God will see that everything works out for your good and on time. King Solomon, one of the wealthiest and wisest men who ever lived gave these instructions: *"Honor Jehovah with thy substance, and with the first fruit of all thine increase (referring to tithing). So shall thy barns be filled with plenty, and thy vats shall overflow with new wine"* (Proverbs 3:9).

By voluntarily giving a tenth of your gross income to spiritual work you can expect financial prosperity and protection from the devourer-i.e. illnesses, thieves, accidents etc., that cost you money and put you in financial binds. Many of the less affluent are inclined to feel that they cannot afford to tithe. They claim that they will do so later when they are in better financial shape, or when some of their financial obligations are met. The devourer will see to it that this will never happen! The time to tithe is when you feel you cannot afford to. In fact you must tell yourself that you cannot afford not too! Obviously your own handling of your finances is inadequate, or you would not be experiencing financial difficulty. Tithing may not make you an overnight millionaire, but it will make you ten times better off than you are! When you learn to give, to loosen your purse strings, you loosen the binding strings of lack. You will find that tithing is the greatest prosperity principle of all. It will improve every area of your life.

Where you give and why you give is equally important to consider as what you give and how your give. You must give cheerfully, for the Lord loves a cheerful giver. Many people spread their tithes around to the poor and needy. This is giving and all giving is good, but it is not tithing. The Bible teaches "bring ye all the tithes into the storehouse--" You should give—expecting a return—and not just because of duty. Many religious people in their piety will proclaim that they are not looking for anything in return. This is contrary to Scriptural teaching, it is contrary to the universal law of giving and receiving, sowing and reaping. If you never receive, you would soon have nothing to give. If you refuse to give, you cannot expect to receive. If you give little, expect to receive little. If you give much, expect to receive much.

There are those who give generously, large gifts to civic, educational and cultural pursuits. This is good too, for all giving is commendable if it is for a good cause. However it is secondary to tithing for there is no promise of a return from divine resources. Many excuse themselves from tithing, saying that Jesus did not emphasize tithing. This is true. Jesus did not emphasize tithing, although it is mentioned twice in his teaching. This was because it was a required part of worship. It was a spiritual requirement. There was no question as to whether worshipers would tithe or not! What the church of today must realize is that tithing is for the good of the individual, it takes nothing away from you that will not be multiplied back unto you. It will bring good in abundance.

The Lord will prosper his own according to their obedience, understanding, and foresight. Abraham was told to get out of his old country and go to a new land which the Lord would show him. As he went forth by faith, the Lord told him to look out before him and he would give him all he could see.

The same promise is given to you and to me. We can have all that we can see. But often it is necessary to get out of the "old country" or the old habits, the old state of mind. You can accomplish this by releasing negative thoughts of lack and powerlessness, old limited ideas, attitudes, fears, and doubts. Sometimes we must relinquish old relationships if they stand in our way. We must look out before us and look up for guidance.

David said, "I will lift my eyes unto the hills from whence cometh my help, my help cometh from the Lord." Look up past poor circumstances, use your imaging power to see all that can be yours. It has often been said that a picture is worth a thousand words. Picture firmly in your mind what you want manifested in your life. See it clearly, and be absolute. Your imaging power is used to create whatever you desire. *"Faith is the substance of things hoped for and the evidence of things not seen"* (Hebrew 11:1). Continuously positively imagine what you want, not what you do not want! Guard against negative thoughts. An example of how you can use the power of your imagination is – for instance, if you need more money, sit, meditate, picture large sums of money, stacks of money: fifties, hundreds and five hundred dollar bills. Do this over and over daily – money will come. Always picture yourself in a prosperous situation instead of one of lack. See yourself in beautiful clothes, a new car, a luxurious home, on wonderful vacations, among wonderful and prosperous people. (Unless, of course, these ideas are contrary to your religious beliefs) To help with imaginary consistency, prepare yourself a scrap book using clippings of beautiful things you would like to have: Floor plans for your dream home, beautiful clothes, a new car, money (play money will serve the purpose) and other things you desire. You may want to visit travel agencies, pick up brochures of luxury vacations. Paste them in your scrap book. Look through your book daily, picture yourself in each situation. All that you can imagine will come to you in both expected and unexpected ways. Whatsoever mankind can imagine in his heart, that can he do (Genesis 11:6).

Perhaps it is love and marriage you desire. Then imagine, in full detail, the type of spouse you want, imagine the wedding you want, the home situation you want, believe that you will have it and you will. Your mental picture will help you become the type of person to attract love. You will become a magnet to draw to you all that you desire. Be careful not to imagine yourself attracting someone who belongs to another. This would be contrary to God's will and bring confusion rather than fulfillment.

We were created in the image (imagination) of God and after his likeness, having the power of imagination unlike any other living creature on earth. This power works to produce for you all that you can imagine. This power or gift is not to be used selfishly. Imagine good about others and for others, then watch changes come about in your life and theirs. See your spouse, children, friends, strangers, neighbors, relatives, co-workers and all with whom you come in contact, in happy prosperous situations. Get to know those around you, find out what they desire, imagine them having it—wish them well and wish them good success. Even apply this principle to your enemies, for as you help create better circumstances and conditions for those around you, quite naturally things will be better for you. Love your neighbor and also love your enemy, do good to them that despitefully use you (Matthew 5:43-44).

Be careful not to be resentful of another's success, or speculate that they "probably obtained it by underhandedness." *"Judge not, that you be not judged, for with what judgment you judge, ye shall be judged"* (Matthew 7:1-2). Instead of envying another's prosperity, imagine yourself in a similar situation of your own. Praise God for the success of others, remembering the lyrics of the song "It is No Secret What God Can Do-what He's done for others, He'll do for you..." But if you are envious of another it is indicative of your being opposed to prosperity – even that of the ungodly and the unjust. The Scriptures teach that God allows his sun to shine on the just and the unjust and His rain to fall on them both. Who are we to object to what God does with what is His?

As you use these principles of prosperity set forth, it is not necessary or wise to discuss what you do with anyone (don't let your left hand know what your right hand is doing). But as you continue to build a better mental picture you will be building a better way of life. Praise God, giving thanks to Him for all His wonderful blessings daily in psalms and songs. Make Psalm 23 a real part of your life. *"The Lord is my shepherd; I shall not want. He maketh me to lie down in green pastures; He leadeth me beside the still waters. He restoreth my soul; He leadeth me in the paths of righteousness for His name sake. Yea, though I walk through the valley of the shadow of death I will fear no evil; For thou art with me; Thy rod and thy staff they comfort me. Thou preparest a table before me in the presence of mine enemies; Thou anointest my head with oil; My cup runneth over. Surely goodness and mercy shall follow me all the days of my life; And I will dwell in the house of the Lord forever.*

Take Ye, Eat.

PEACE: HARMONY WITH GOD'S UNIVERSE

When we are troubled and upset it is usually not so much 'what' is the matter as 'who' is the matter. If you feel frustrated by another person, for whatever reason you are not happy with a situation, you need first to realize that the other person is not the problem but how you feel about the person is your problem. Once this is realized, you have the power to change your feelings if you will. Denying or ignoring the feeling will only generate additional problems, possibly to the detriment of ourselves and others. Psychologists and others concerned with mental health believe that our feelings have much to do with our mental health. Feelings of long-standing, suppressed emotion, and misplaced feelings contribute to mental illnesses. Once we recognize and identify the feeling, we can begin to put it aside. Jealousy, for example, reveals a need to re-evaluate one's feeling of self-worth and come to understand that we are special in our own right, that we are important, loved, and a direct expression of an omnipotent God. The more we are centered in the realization that we are beloved of God, we can free ourselves from all negative feelings, and hold on to the good ones. Sometimes we experience the feeling of being cheated, that someone close to us is not doing their fair share, or that they may get credit for something they didn't do. Peter had this concern about John, the beloved disciple of Jesus. Jesus had instructed Peter to follow him but Peter was concerned right away about what John was going to do. Jesus response to Peter was: "What is that to thee? follow thou me" (John 21:22). Perhaps it would greatly help maintain inward peace if we could apply this to our concerns about what others are doing or going to do, or what we feel they should be doing, or what they should not be doing for that matter. You do what you're supposed to be doing. The fear that someone can take away that which is rightfully ours reveals a need for greater faith in God. We can cast away our anxieties as we affirm that "greater is He that is within me than he that is in the world." It is not wise to hold on to negative feelings about others, regardless of who they are, what they do or say. We can continue to love them, realizing that they belong to God even as we belong to God. Our job is not to condemn or to condone but to follow Christ. *"The earth is the Lord's, the fullness thereof, the world and they that dwell therein"* (Psalms 24:1).

There are indeed those around who will try to put stumbling blocks in your way but you can affirm *"you meant evil against me; but God meant it for good"*(Genesis 50:20). It may not be easy to look beyond adverse circumstances and situations and see the good. But God can make your stumbling blocks into stepping stones. Every circumstance and situation teaches a valuable lesson. When you learn your lesson, you receive your blessing! Think of a time in your life when a negative situation turned out to be a great benefit. The song writer said, "through many dangers, toils and snares I have already come, twas grace that brought me safe thus far and grace shall lead me on." Look beyond appearances and know that God is still in control. Your faith in God's loving presence will guide you triumphantly through seemingly impossible situations. God specializes in things that seem impossible. God will bring about only good to those who put their trust in him.

"For we know that all things work together for good to them that love the Lord and are called according to his purpose" (Romans 8:28).

There is no need to focus on the problem but on the solution, not on the conflict but on the answer, not on the crisis but on the Christ, not on the imperfect, but on the perfect, not on the guile, but on the guide. Everyone wants happy and harmonious lives. We want our relations with other people to be peaceful. This is possible if we let the love of God find expression through us. We have the indwelling power of God to reject feelings of discord and project feelings of accord. We have the power to overlook disagreements and differences. We can focus our attention on the likeness we share with one another, and with our creator God, in all that is fine and good.

One of the greatest sources of difficulty in interpersonal relationships is to honestly deal with feelings. If you are despondent, worried and upset over some situation in your life, it will accomplish no good to deny your feelings. Yet if you observe, you will notice that a great deal of effort is made to ignore or deny feelings. Frequently you will hear statements such as "let's keep our feelings out of this" or "why don't you keep your feelings to yourself?" or you hear this useless observation "it's silly to feel that way" or the advice "oh, don't feel that way about it." One very popular song gives this advice "smile when you're feeling blue." Also you may observe that when feelings are honestly disclosed, it is usually after the fact. Feelings are seldom discussed in the present tense, but either past feelings or anticipated future feelings. Feelings not acknowledged or dealt with properly are a source of discontentment.

Feelings cannot be controlled by ignoring them or denying them. In fact, when you attempt to deny or ignore them you are allowing them to control you. Feelings are one source through which we can process information regarding relationships with others and situations in our lives. You put yourself at the mercy of a situation if you are not in tune with what is happening. Feelings are signals that should be checked out, so that you may get a hold on things before they get a hold on you. This is not advocating that you should live by feelings, but that we may put our feelings in subjection. One very common feeling that everyone experiences at one time or another is sorrow. Maybe it is sickness in your life, with its suffering, its expenses and its uncertainty. Or it could be that death has struck within your family with its agony and pain. Perhaps it is that your fondest dream has been shattered by a Judas in your life. You may have asked the question, "Lord, why me?" This is a good question to ask. You need not feel guilty for "questioning God" as some suppose. It is only in presenting a question that you can receive an answer. Then listen for God's still small voice speaking within you. There is no one that can answer the question "Lord, why me?" but the Lord. Others can suggest that it was because of this or that, but they truly don't know.

"If any man seeks wisdom, let him ask of God" (James 1:19). It is wisdom that will move you to present questions that an all wise loving God is ready, willing and able to answer rather than resorting to human reasoning. Many people tend to reason that God is punishing them for some sin they have committed. If this was true it would be foolish to pray for God to help you. If God's main purpose was to punish you for sin, your very life could have been taken, for the "wages of sin is death" not just suffering.

God is more interested in blessing you than in punishing you! The truth is that most of our problems we bring on ourselves - God did not send them. It is, however, true that He allows trials to come into our lives. Unfortunately, it is the only way to get our attention sometimes. He will permit you to suffer for a short time, that you may turn to Him and realize that He is a rewarder of them that diligently seek Him. It is not God's will that anyone should suffer.

You have immediate access to peace, love, joy, health, happiness, prosperity, success, vitality and completeness. All these things are your divine heritage as a child of the most High King. Jesus declared unto his followers *"Peace I leave with you, my peace I give unto you; not as the world giveth, give I unto you. Let not your heart be troubled, neither let it be afraid"* (John 14:27). The Comforter, the indwelling Spirit of God, is all powerful and all knowing. He knows your every need. He will lead you and keep you in perfect peace. We may take detours along the way, choose to travel rough roads, not following the way he has made, but the Holy Spirit is ever present to restore and to reveal to us the way to our highest good. God's power is ever present to bring peace.

Some people fall into the trap of affirming discord. They often say things like "I don't understand my mother" or "I don't understand my father," "my wife," "my husband," "my brother," "my sister," "my boss" etc. Without realizing it, they are inviting misunderstanding, they are preparing for misunderstandings and confusion to be a part of their lives. If you will allow God's compassion and wisdom to be released from within you, you will have the ability to understand. Proclaim understanding rather than misunderstanding. See all things in a loving way. Release fears, doubt, and hostility and hold to trust, love, and harmony in all of your dealings.

If you are at the crossroads in your life, unsure of which path to take, let go and let God direct your path, knowing that His way is sure and He will show you the right way. He will guide you in making the right decision. Trust God. If you're concerned about a loved one, a son, a daughter who has gone wayward, remember that those whom you love are loved even more by God. He is with them as their ever present help as he is with you. God is omniscient, omnipresent, and omnipotent. His mercies endureth forever, He is a God of love, He is creator and sustainer of all the universe. By wisdom the Lord founded the earth itself and established the heavens. He set into motion the laws of cause and effect. He designed the solar system with its revolving planets, and then constructed the atom in like manner with a number of electrical particles, protons, neutrons and electrons, each in its special space location, each performing with precision! Humanity is yet discovering the complexity of God's creation, the precision, and harmony. It is good to learn the way of things and work in accord with them. The sun itself shines for you, but you must rise when the sun rises. It will not rise when you rise. The mighty ocean tides flow for you, but you must flow with the tide. To be at peace is to be in harmony with

God, man and creation. *"And God said, Let us make man in our image, after our likeness; and let them have dominion over the fish of the sea, and over the fowl of the air, and over the cattle, and over all the earth, and over every creeping thing that creepeth upon the earth.*

So God created man in his own image, in *the image of God created he him; male and female created he them"* (Genesis 1:26-27). Genesis, the book of beginnings, teaches us that mankind (male and female) were created in the image and after the likeness of God and they were given dominion over all the earth and all that was within the earth. However, God determined how things were to operate. God set the laws of nature in motion: He separated the light from the darkness; called light day and the darkness night; he divided the waters from the waters; he divided and set the boundaries of the waters and the land; he commanded that trees, vegetation, etc. would yield fruit whose seed was in itself; he made the lights of the heavens, the greater to rule the day and the lesser to rule the night; the stars to be for signs and for seasons. He determined how all his creatures should exist and function within the laws of nature. Adam and Eve violated the law of peace and harmony, thus bringing about shame and discord for themselves. Nevertheless, even then our Heavenly Father was watching over them. He planned a means for man to overcome, from the beginning. The seed of the woman would conquer and become victorious over all" (Genesis 3: 15). Man was to work and keep the land. This is God's divine plan. If we only realize that God has always been near when we need him, we could, like Charles H. Gabriel, say, "Why should I feel discouraged, why should the shadows come, why should my heart be lonely and long for heav'n and home, when Jesus is my portion, my constant friend is he, His eye is on the sparrow, and I know He watches me. Let not your heart be troubled His tender word I hear, and resting on His goodness, I lose my doubts and fears; Tho by the path he leadeth but one step I may see; His eye is on the sparrow, and I know He watches me, His eye is on the sparrow, and I know he watches me."

SALVATION: YOUR ETERNAL LIFE NOW

Eternal life begins now for you if you believe; that God sent His son Jesus Christ to die for the sins of the world; that he was crucified and died on the cross at Calvary; that he was buried in Joseph's new tomb; and arose on the third day with all power in his hand. Salvation is the free gift from God to those who believe. There is then no longer any question about our eternal destiny. Eternal means forevermore and not a gift that is given today then retrieved tomorrow or next week or year because of something you did or did not do that upset God. God is not like mankind, He is all-knowing and knew what you were going to do before you did it. The Bible also teaches that His mercies endure forever! "God so loved the world that he gave his only begotten son, that whosoever believeth in him should not perish, but have everlasting life" (John 3:16).

If you were to ask some, what must one do to have everlasting life, undoubtedly you would receive one or more of the following answers:

To be saved you must obey the ten commandments.
To be saved you must join a church and become active in its work.
To be saved you must follow Christ's example of doing good.
To be saved you must repent and be baptized.
To be saved you must walk upright.
To be saved you must live a Christian life.
To be saved you must study your Bible.

To be saved you must give up worldly things.
To be saved you must tarry until the Holy Ghost comes.
To be saved you must be converted and get religion.
To be saved you must first love everybody.

Although all these things are perhaps reflective of various aspects of the life and experiences of those who have been saved, they are not the simple Bible answer to salvation (see John 3:16). *Salvation* is *a gift to the believer.*

The Bible makes it very plain that we cannot do anything to earn or win salvation- not by anything we have done, can do, intend to do, try to do, or desire to do. Salvation is a free gift. The Bible teaches us that we were not good enough nor can we become good enough to merit eternal life, but it is altogether because of God's love and mercy. No one can be made right in God's sight by keeping the command-ments. For the more we truly come to understand God's laws, the clearer it becomes that we aren't obeying them; his laws serve to make us see that we are sinners. God says he will accept us and declare us not guilty, we receive justification for our sins if we trust Jesus to take away our sins (Romans 3). God, being rich in mercy, loved us so much that even though we were spiritually dead in our sins, He gave us back our lives again when Christ was raised from the dead. We are now risen with him. It is only by his grace we have been saved and made righ-teous with the Father. Thus we have been commanded to be righteous even as he is righteous.

Who then can be called "righteous"? The morally upright? The faithful church member? The cheerful giver? The great theologians? The teachers of the law? The keepers of the law? Of course not, none of these - although all of these are products of the righteous; they are not producers of the righteous. Products do not produce producers, but producers produce products!

Henry Ford produced automobiles. Automobiles did not produce Henry Ford. However, had Henry Ford failed to produce he would not have come to be known as the producer he was.

Who then are the righteous? The righteous are those counted righteous by God. *"By faith Abel offered unto God a more excellent sacrifice than Cain by which he obtained witness that he was righteous."*(Hebrew 11:4) *"By faith Noah, being warned of God of things not seen as yet, moved with fear prepared an ark to the saving of his house, by which he condemned the world, and become heir of the righteousness which is by faith"* (Hebrew 11:7). *"And he (Abraham) believed in the LORD; and he counted it to him for righteousness"* (Genesis 15:6). *"For by grace are ye saved through faith; and that not of yourselves, it is the gift of God - Not of works lest any man should boast"* (Ephesians 2:8-9). These passages of the Scriptures make it all very simple. You are counted righteous by God because of your faith in God to make you righteous in him. For without faith it is impossible to please God! Furthermore anything that is not of faith is sin!

It seems as though humans, in their religious vanity, have too often thought of the righteousness of God to be limited to, or applicable to the morality of man. Man's morals should indeed be in accord with God's laws and principles set forth. Even before Moses' presentation of the ten commandments, God's laws were in operation - from the beginning of creation. His laws are good, they are productive, they are eternal and true. It is the law which causes a bare branch to bring forth green leaves; it is God's law which changes the caterpillar into a butterfly; it is God's law which causes the vapors to rise from the waters and to fall again to water the earth; it is the law of God which causes the lightning's flashes and thunders to roll; As we come to understand and discover these laws, we find them to be for our good. It was the discovery of one of these laws which made electricity a reality to us. It was the discovery of one of these laws that makes it possible for great ships to stay afloat on the seas, planes to glide through the air, and humans to travel out into space.

It is God's law that declares Jesus Christ as our righteousness, it is the discovery of this truth that brings to us eternal life. Because of God's kindness, we have been saved by his power divine, saved to new life sublime. Therefore none of us can take credit for our salvation, not even in part. This is the simple, plain truth of the Bible doctrine on salvation. Many Christians worry about teaching this simple truth because they fear that some will take this teaching to mean that it doesn't matter what we do, whether we choose to continue in sin or not since our salvation has nothing to do with our works. What foolish reasoning! When individuals have truly accepted Christ into their lives, they would have no desire to continue in sinful, lustful lives; but when one has only claimed that they have accepted Christ, this attitude would prevail. Jesus Christ stated that whoever said that they loved him but would not keep his commandments, they were liars. They had not accepted him at all. God cannot be fooled!

If Christ has indeed been received into their lives, he is able to change them, they become new creatures, old things are passed away. If we have accepted Jesus Christ as our Lord and Savior, God has accepted us as his righteous ones.

Man

A pure reflection of perfect love, life and liberty,
That is what man was made to be.
God is love, and all that is good,
All that is or ever shall be is of God.
He is Alpha and Omega, He is the great I am,
These reflections of God upon creation, became Adam.
Man is God's reflection of love upon the earth,
A reflection of life from God's own sweet breath.
A pure reflection of love, life and liberty,
That is what man was made to be.
The reflection was shattered,

When man partook of the forbidden tree.
The creator God, of who's reflection is man,
Clothed Himself in flesh and began
To pick up the pieces of that shattered reflection,
To put them together again in absolute perfection.

As you come to understand this great truth, the best of life is stirred to greater fullness. As you open your mind to truth, and rejoice in all things God gives, you will find life and find abundance of all good things in your life. You can know that wherever you go, whatever you do, you are alive with God's Spirit, you are alert, you are strengthened by his might. You can be assured that you shall be like a tree planted by rivers or waters, whose leaf shall not wither, and that whatsoever you do will prosper. You can begin to realize that every cell of your being is filled with life in abundance. You can begin to have a new vision of the world, your work, and the importance of your place in the scheme of things.

"Awake, O sleeper and Christ shall give you light" (Ephesians 5:14). Keep your mind active and alert by looking at life with enthusiasm. Let the intelligence of God be expressed through you. You can know that your mind is one with God. You can release all doubts and fears, knowing that the Spirit of God within you will reveal to you the way to reach your goals and how to achieve your objectives. Trust God's divine spirit to furnish you with power, knowledge and strength, to be all he would have you to be. Don't sleep on the job and Christ shall give you light. This is the promise of salvation. Remember your eternal life begins the moment you believe. You don't have to wait for "pie in the sky by and by." Jesus said to the malefactor on the cross, the one who expressed faith in Jesus to save, "This day thou shall be with me in paradise." This man represents all those who come by faith. You can be with Christ this day, right now, in paradise. This simple prayer prayed in faith - will bring you salvation right now.

"Dear God, I confess that I am a sinner and I am unable to save myself. I ask your forgiveness for my sins and confess that Jesus is the Christ. I invite you to come into my life right now, make me a new creature. Amen." It is now up to you to have the faith that God has this moment made you a new creature. Begin to study his word, and walk therein. Apply his word to your life.

Early every morning, each and every day, ask the Lord to lead and guide you all along the way. If you follow the leading of the Holy Spirit, you will not stray.

SUCCESS: SEVEN STEPS FROM WHERE YOU ARE

"*This book of the law shall not depart out of thy mouth, but thou shalt meditate therein day and night, that thou mayest observe to do according to all that is written therein; For then thou shalt make thy way prosperous, and then thou shalt have good success*" (Joshua 1:8). These are the words the Lord spoke unto Joshua. Likewise these are words the Lord is speaking to his people today- be strong, courageous, faithful and true. You can be successful, no matter where you are now or what you're doing, you're only seven steps away from having what you want to have, doing what you want to do and being what you want to be. These seven laws of success have been used by every successful man and woman, whether they were followed knowingly or unknowingly.

Seven Steps to Success

1. Be definite in what your goal is and identify it clearly.

2. Prepare yourself mentally, study.

3. Keep yourself as physically fit as possible.

4. Work toward your goal with all your might.

5. Concentrate, plan, think.

6. Be confident, don't give up in the face of adversity.

7. Have faith that God will bring it to pass.

(From *Serve The Lord With Gladness* by Lena Williams McMillon)
Let us examine these steps one by one. First it is necessary to identify
your goal so you will know it when you reach it! If you were planning a
vacation in the Bahamas it would be necessary to say so, to be specific
when purchasing your ticket to travel. Likewise you need to be specific
as to your destination on your journey to reaching your goal. Write it
down, remind yourself often of your ultimate destination, share your
goal planning with others. You should know where you are headed and
why.

Secondly, begin to prepare yourself mentally, study, begin "pack-
ing" away information that you will need in reaching your destination,
and that you will need when you reach your destination. If it is necessary to go to school, or enter some special program of study - do it!
There is much information available at your library on just about every
subject you can think of- use it. If you are already working and simply
wish to move up in your present area of employment, you can do much
toward promoting yourself by your attitude. Volunteer to help in the
area of your interest. Learn all you can about the work you want to do.
Be alert for opportunities to serve.

Thirdly, keep yourself as physically fit as possible. Exercise and nu-
trition are important to your success. If your body is healthy, in good
shape, and well nourished, you will be more energetic, you will feel
better about yourself, others will feel better about you, and you will,
more than likely, feel like investing that extra time required to attain
your goal. It stands to reason that when you don't have to respond constantly to physical discomforts, sickness, aches, pains etc., you will be
able to concentrate your efforts on attaining your goal.

Fourth, work toward your goal with all your might. Keep your eyes
on your goal. Be constant, persevering, consistent, and conscientious.
The lyrics of one popular hymn say: "Life is like a mountain railroad,
with an engineer that's brave; we must make the run successful, from

the cradle to the grave; watch the curves, the hills, the tunnels, never falter, never quail; Keep your hand upon the throttle, and your eye upon the rail." You must keep your attention directed toward attainment. Often you find hard-working people working hard at too many things and never knowing exactly what they truly want to do. They usually become "a jack of all trades, and master of none." Stick with your decision, work in the area of your interest, even if it means sometimes working for less monetary reward. Remember money is not always a measuring stick for success. You should find pleasure in your work, and work in your pleasure. Few people find this combination.

Fifth, you must concentrate, plan, think, concentrate, plan, think. You will have to do much more than wishing, hoping or even praying in order to attain your goal. You need to think about what you're about to say before you say it. You need to think about who you're talking too before you talk too much. You need to plan your strategies well. But keep one thing in mind, it will never truly profit you anything if your plan is to ·walk over someone else or to mistreat someone else in order to reach your destination. *"Be not deceived, God is not mocked, for whatsoever a man soweth, that shall he also reap"* (Galatians 6:7).

Sixth, be confident, and don't give up in the face of adversity. Sometimes when problems arise, they seem like roadblocks in our way, but instead of allowing them to become stumbling blocks, you can make them into stepping stones toward your success! Rather than panicking when some problems arise, learn to be calm, steady and in control. Look at the situation and try to see where it can be beneficial to you, and not only to you but also unto others. By so doing, many enemies have been turned into friends. This is the significance of Matthew 5:44: "Love your enemies, do good to them that hate you, and pray for them who despitefully use you, and persecute you. Remember it is more profitable to make friends out of enemies than enemies out of friends."

Seventh, have faith that God will bring it to pass. Hebrew 11:1 says that *"Faith is the substance of things hoped for, the evidence of things not seen."* Just as a butterfly emerges from a caterpillar's chrysalis, faith emerges from hope. Faith is one of the most powerful forces on earth. It is a power that will catapult one to attainment. There is nothing impossible to man if he has faith. A good example is the report Caleb brought back to Moses and Aaron of the inhabitants of the land of Canaan as opposed to the other men who went with him. *"Caleb stilled the people before Moses, and said, Let us go up at once, and possess it; for we are well able to overcome it. But the men who went up with him said, We are not able to go up against the people; for they are stronger than we"* (Numbers 13:30-31). They told Moses *"we came unto the land which thou sentest us, and surely it floweth with milk and honey; and this is the fruit of it. Nevertheless, the people are strong that dwell in the land, and the cities are walled, and very great"*(vss. 27 and 28) Theirs was a statement of fear rather than one of faith. Fear will stop you from going after what you want, even when you see it. But faith says you can do it!

"Blessed is the man who walketh not in the counsel of the ungodly, nor standeth in the way of sinners, nor sitteth in the seat of the scornful. But his delight is in the law of the Lord; and in his law doth he meditate day and night. And he shall be like a tree planted by the rivers of water, that bringeth forth its fruit in its season; its leaf also shall not wither; and whatsoever he doeth shall prosper. The ungodly are not so, but are like the chaff which the wind driveth away. Therefore, the ungodly shall not stand in the judgment, nor sinners in the congregation of the righteous. For the Lord knoweth the way of the righteous; but the way of the ungodly shall perish" (Psalm 1). This passage of Scripture represents two types of men, two ways of reasoning, and two destinies. Take ye, Eat.

POWER: NATURAL AND SUPERNATURAL

What is power? Funk & Wagnall defines power as: the ability to act; capability; potential capacity; strength or force actually put forth; the right, ability, or capacity to exercise control; a mental or physical faculty; any form of energy available for doing work.

As we look around us we are aware of various powers: political power, technological power, societal powers, and invisible powers. Everyone has some power whether or not they recognize it or whether or not they have thought about it. Each person has influence one way or another over someone or something. The power referred to here is in the natural realm of everyday living which includes; legitimate power, the power which is given to leaders, the right to make some decisions concerning others and often for others; affective power, the power which is earned as a result of the high level of respect others have for the person; expertise power, the power granted when one demonstrates a high level of knowledge in a particular area; psychological power, the power which results generally from rewards - monetary, recognition, praise, superior communication skills as speaking, writing, or social sensitivity skills. Of course there is also coercive power where force or threats are used to accomplish goals.

In determining your personal effectiveness power you should look at each of these variables. The area in which you find weakness you can begin to redirect your energies as necessary to bring about the desired results. Others are more likely to follow the person they respect and trust. They are more likely to follow the person who has expertise or knows what he's talking about. They are more likely to follow the person who shows love, loyalty, respect and concern to his fellowman. They are more likely to follow the person who is assertive, self-confident and willing to take the initiative. They are more likely to follow the person who possesses effective communication skills. Communication is one skill that is most vital to leadership and power. This includes having the ability to empathize with and understand others, attentiveness in listening to others and the ability to communicate well, both orally and in writing. Intuition is also a power each person possesses in some degree. Our intuitive powers can lead us to the very inwardness of life. Intuition is inward and immediate, it enables us to receive inspiration of the Almighty God and to experience unity with God. Great powers in science and in technology have been gained, but unfortunately these powers have been used for destructive purposes. Comparatively, little advancement has been made toward the ultimate happiness and well-being of man through science and technology. Albert Einstein, one of the men we have to thank most for the release of atomic energy, reportedly stated: "The unleashed power of the atom has changed everything except our way of thinking. Thus we are drifting toward a catastrophe beyond comparison. We shall require substantially a new manner of thinking if mankind is to survive" *(Nuclear Weapons and the Conflict of Conscience,* 1962). We must be careful not to extend our reliance upon scientific and technological power too far. Each person must make decisions and act upon them.

Life forces us to make choices and to act on the basis of our own values. Our choices and conduct are our own. They are within our power.

So far we have discussed natural powers that we use daily in our natural world. However, supernatural powers exist in the spirit world. They are also ours to use to our good and the good of others, or to be used to our detriment. All too often when we think of supernatural powers, we immediately think of the powers of witchcraft or sorcery, but the gifts of the spirit are supernatural for they are not of man but of God.

We wrestle not against flesh and blood, not against people, but against spirit beings, evil rulers of the unseen world, and against wicked spirits in the spirit world. There are unseen forces with which we must contend. To do so, the Bible teaches that we must put on the whole armor of God to be able to stand. You will need to be equipped with the spirit of truth, peace, understanding, faith, God's Word and the salvation of righteousness.

You must be prayerful, watchful, and persevering. Along with spiritual "armor" for your protection, you are given authority to rule and super-rule by the Lord's mighty power within you.

The Bible gives insight into the spirit world. Hundreds of Scriptures reveal various spirit beings 'that inhabit the material around us. There are many kinds of spirits revealed. Scriptures are full of the supernatural. The natural world and the spiritual co-exist, there is only one step which separates them. We refer to this as death. Scriptures mention angelic beings of the spirit world: Seraphim (Isaiah 6: 1-7), Cherubim (Ezekiel 1:5), (Genesis 3:24) Zoa (Revelation 4:6-9), Spirit horses and chariot drivers (Romans 1:20) (2 Corinthians 1:4) (Zechariah 1:8-11), Archangels (I Thessalonians 4: 16) (Revelation 12:7-9), and numerous other Scriptures mention spirit beings. Angels are wise, patient, holy, glorious, immortal, heavenly beings, that help individuals, strengthen in trial, lead sinners to gospel workers, minister before God, bind Satan, receive departed spirits, bring answers to prayers, and perform many other services for God and man. They are not to be worshipped but are to be judged and ruled by saints. They are organized into powers and principalities. There are also fallen angels- there are two classes: those bound and those still loose with Satan (Rev. 12:7-12) (Ephesians

6:10-17). Angels have real, tangible bodies and body parts like men. There are also devils, demons, and unclean spirits. The devil has an angelic body and cannot enter into anyone, but demons are disembodied spirits who operate through possession of men and beast. Although intelligent and wise, demons are evil (1 Timothy 4: I) (I Kings 22:22-24). They are powerful and have emotions (Acts 8:7). They possess people and cause dumbness, deafness, blindness, lunacy, mania, fits, lust, sicknesses, diseases, deceptions, fear, false doctrines, violence, and every evil they possibly can cause to man and toward God. They can seem friendly, go out and come back into man, imitate the departed dead, and can do many things when in possession of a body. They have no power to act without a body.

This is but a small mention of the vast spirit world which co-exists with the natural, but it is necessary to be aware of what we contend with and to also realize we have the power to overcome, for we have the victory in the name of Jesus!

The redeemed of the Lord have the power by the name of Jesus to cast out demons, and to do all kinds of mighty works by faith. Faith is a spiritual power to be used skillfully against evil spiritual powers.

We must deal with spiritual beings with spiritual weapons. Use truth, the Word of God, prayer, faith, courage, understanding, love and peace to overcome evil. To have power with God and with mankind, we must first and foremost realize that it is not mankind with which we contend, but the powers of the spirit world that provoke the unwise to do evil. Overcome evil with your good.

"As many as received him, to them gave he power to become the children of God even to them that believe on his name"(John 1:12). The helmet of salvation offers protection forevermore against all the wiles of the devil. Total salvation includes deliverance from sickness, disease, poverty, confusion, hate, jealousy, fear and even death. God has given you the power of attorney to act in authority. This power must be

claimed by faith, then faith must be acted upon, fearlessly and boldly. According to the promise of Jesus, all believers have power to do the works he himself did, and even greater works. The world is hungry for manifestations of this supernatural power, for healing, answers to prayers, to overcome all manner of evil, but alas, there is much apostasy in the church, a leaning toward human understanding and human reasoning, rejecting the supernatural power of God and relying on human power alone. We have been warned that human powers alone are no match for satanic forces. Until Christians begin acting by the power of the Holy Spirit as Christ did, they will remain spiritual babies. God has not changed, His word has not changed, Sin is still sin, Satan is still Satan, and faith still has the power to overcome. According to your faith so be it unto you - even as you will.

RICHES & HONOUR: GIFTS FROM GOD

"And I have also given thee that which thou hast not asked, both riches and honour: so that there shall not be any among the kings like unto thee all thy days"(I Kings 3:13).

Solomon did not pray for riches and honor, rather he prayed for understanding. We would be wise to likewise pray for understanding of the ways of things and of people, and as we act with understanding in the affairs of our life, with right principles, both riches and honor will follow.

Many devout religious people have thought that riches and honor were of the world, and not to be desired by godly people. They have felt that money was a lure of Satan, and seldom if ever saw it as being a gift of God. I wonder if it is this belief that keeps many believers from rising above poverty level! This concept is a trick of Satan to keep God's people down, for Satan knows, as you and I know, that **money is power.** However, it is power to do good or evil. Money used for good is an honor, but money used for evil is a shame unto you, for *"where your treasure is there will your heart be also"* (Matthew 6:21). It is how you choose to use your money that counts, whether it is much or little.

Scriptures bear out that God has delighted in blessing His people with much riches. Abraham was a very rich man, as was also Isaac, Jacob, David, Job, Joseph, Moses, and on and on the list goes. God is still passing out blessings!

There is no magical formula for acquiring riches and honor but that of understanding, wisdom, self-discipline, love and reverence for God. The book of Proverbs, attributed to Solomon, points the way in numerous passages. I have chosen a few to share with you.

"True humility and respect for the Lord lead a man to riches, honor and long life" (Proverbs 22: 4).

"A man who loves pleasure becomes poor; wine and luxury are not the way to riches" (Proverbs 21:17).

"Hard work brings prosperity; playing around brings poverty" (Proverbs 28:19).

Do you know a hard-working 'man? He shall be successful and stand before kings" (Proverbs 22:29).

"Get the facts at any price, and hold on tightly to all the good sense you can get" (Proverbs 23:23).

"Develop your business first before building your house" (Proverbs 24:27).

"Any enterprise is built by wise planning, becomes strong through common sense, and profits wonderfully by keeping abreast of the facts" (Proverbs 24:3).

"When you help the poor you are lending to the Lord - and he pays wonderful interest on your loan!" (Proverbs 19:17).

"Greed causes fighting; trusting God leads to prosperity" (Proverbs 28:25).

"Steady plodding brings prosperity; hasty speculation brings poverty" (Proverbs 21:5).

"Many favors are showered on those who please the King" (Proverbs 16:15).

"Despise God's Word and find yourself in trouble. Obey it and succeed" (Proverbs 13:13).

"The Lord preserves the upright but ruins the plans of the wicked" (Proverbs 22:12).

"Never abandon a friend - either yours or your father's. Then you won't need to go to a distant relative for help in your time of need" (Proverbs 27:10).

"Charm can be deceptive and beauty doesn't last, but a woman who fears and reverences God shall be greatly praised" (Proverbs 31:30).

"Self-control means controlling the tongue! A quick retort can ruin everything" (Proverbs 13:3).

"Work brings profit; talk brings poverty" (Proverbs 14:23).

"A wise man holds his tongue. Only a fool blurts out everything he knows; that only leads to sorrow and trouble" (Proverbs 10:14).

"A wise man restrains his anger and overlooks insults. This is to his credit" (Proverbs 19:11).

"If you are looking for advice stay away from fools" (Proverbs 14:7).

"Wise men are praised for their wisdom; fools are despised for their folly" (Proverbs 14:24).

"Be with wise men and become wise. Be with evil men and become evil" (Proverbs 13:20).

"Don't envy godless men; don't even enjoy their company" (Proverbs 24:1).

"Discretion shall preserve thee, understanding shall keep thee" (Proverbs 2:3).

"In all thy ways acknowledge him and he shall direct thy paths" (Proverbs 3:6).

"Honour the Lord with thy substance, and with the first fruits of all thine increase So shall thy barns be filled with plenty, and thy presses shall burst out with new wine" (Proverbs 3:9-10).

"He *becometh poor that dealeth with a slack hand; But the hand of the diligent maketh rich*" (Proverbs 10:4).

"*Poverty and shame shall be to him that refuseth instruction: but he that regardeth reproof shall be honoured*" (Proverbs 13:18).

"*A man's gift maketh room for him, and bringeth him before great men*" (Proverbs 18:16).

"*Love not sleep, lest thou come to poverty; open thine eyes, and thou shalt be satisfied with bread*" (Proverbs 20:13).

"*So shall the knowledge of wisdom be unto thy soul: when thou hast found it, then there shall be reward, and thy expectation shall not be cut off*" (Proverbs 24:14).

"*He that giveth to the poor shall not lack; but he that hideth his eyes shall have many a curse*" (Proverbs 28:27).

"*A man is known by his actions. An evil man lives an evil life; a good man lives a godly life*" (Proverbs 21:8).

"*A mirror reflects a man's face, but what he is really like is shown by the kind of friends he chooses*" (Proverbs 27:19).

Honor and riches are gifts from God.

Meditations from Psalms →

Gleanings from Ecclesiastes →

MEDITATIONS FROM PSALMS

To meditate is to reflect upon, ponder and to study, also to mutter-speak repeatedly and continually. It is to think deeply, to believe and receive.

Psalms 23:1: "The Lord is my shepherd, I shall not want."

Psalms 24:1: "The earth is the Lord's, the fullness thereof, the world and they who dwell therein."

Psalms 27:1: "The Lord is my light and my salvation; whom shall I fear?"

Psalms 75:6,7: "For promotion cometh neither from the east, nor from the west, nor from the south. But God is the judge; He putteth down one, and setteth up another."

Psalms 84:11: "For the Lord is a sun and shield. The Lord will give grace and glory. No good thing will He withhold from them that walk uprightly."

Psalms 37:45: "Delight thyself also in the Lord and He shall give thee the desires of thine heart. Commit thy way unto the lord, trust in Him also and He shall bring it to pass."

Psalms 145:17-19: "The Lord is righteous in all His ways and holy in all His works." Whatever He does is right.

Don't presume to judge or limit God by thinking 'that's not fair or that's not right! How dare you!

Gleanings from Ecclesiastes

The author of the book of Ecclesiastes is Solomon, son of David. His theme is Man's Reasoning about Life. These writings represent the world-view of one of the wisest men – who knew there was and is and ever shall be a holy and righteous God who brings everything into judgment.

Solomon points out the futility and vanity of earthly things apart from God. He declares that "All is vanity." The futility of being born, only to suffer, to toil, hoping for gain, only to die and leave it all. He talks about the ceaseless cycle of earthly experiences, Chapter 1:9 says "The thing that hath been, it is that which shall be done; and there is no new thing under the sun." One generation passes and another generation comes along. The sun rises and the sun goes down. The wind blows this way and that, then returns to its circuit. The rivers all flow unto the sea, yet the sea is not full. The place from where the rivers flow, they return to again. Life is a ceaseless cycle. We need not strive for anything. We are to fear (reverence praise, glorify) God and live according to His precepts, this is our duty (Eccles. 12:13).

PROMISES OF GOD

"Seek ye first the Kingdom of God, and His righteousness, and all these things shall be added unto you" (Matthew 6:33).

"Ask and it shall be given, seek and ye shall find, knock and it shall be opened unto you" (Luke 11:9).

"For the Lord is a sun and shield; the Lord will give grace and glory: No good thing will He withhold from them that walk uprightly" (Psalm 84:11).

"Promotion cometh neither from the east nor from the west, nor from the south. But God is the Judge; He putteth down one, and setteth up another" (Psalm 75: 6,7).

"Delight thyself also in the Lord; and He shall give thee the desires of thine heart" (Psalm 37: 6,7).

"Trust in the Lord with all thine heart; and lean not unto thine own understanding. In all thy ways acknowledge Him, and He shall direct thy paths" (Proverbs 3: 5,6).

CONT. GLEANINGS FROM ECCLESIASTES

His promise to us is to "seek first the kingdom of God and His righteousness, and all these things shall be added unto you" (Matt. 6:33).

"And I say unto you ask and it shall be given, seek and ye shall find, knock and it shall be opened unto you" (Luke 11:9).

No more striving after the wind, toiling, suffering to acquire things only to die – to leave it all. This offers little joy. However, the joy of the Lord is forever. The blessings and benefits that await those willing to take God at His word and know that successful living, abundant living, love, happiness, good health, power and prosperity are yours.

John 10:10: "I am come that they may have life, and that they might have it more abundantly."

LOVE: THE GREATEST OF ALL GIFTS

Reverend H. G. McMillon Jr., B.S., M.S. W.,
Pastor Pleasant Green Baptist Church; Omaha, Nebraska

"Now abideth faith, hope, and charity; but the greatest of these is charity" (I Cor. 13:13, KJV)

"In a word there are three things that last forever; faith, hope, and love; but the greatest of them all is love"(I Cor. 13:13 NEB).

Eros, Philia, or Agape? What is Paul talking about in this writing?

This is an age in which there is much talk about love, and it leads one to wonder about the society in which we live. It would appear to me that what the world is calling love is eros - sensuality, lust, strong physical attraction between male and female. This is erotic love. This is not the love Paul was talking about in this passage of Scripture.

If Paul was not talking about eros, or erotic love- then could he have been referring to philia - family love or brotherly love? I would suggest not, simply because family love or brotherly love is based upon relationship or blood lineage rather than spiritual or Christian principle. Friendly love was not the subject either because it suggests something superficial and shallow. The love

Paul declares to be the greatest is much deeper than any love described so far.

The love Paul is referring to is agape love- divine love-a love that is caring, sharing, giving, a love that is unselfish, one that is not based on reciprocity.

Divine love is not a possession of the natural (unconverted) person, but is of a supernatural source - God. God is ready to make this love available upon one's acceptance of Him as the Lord of his life – unconditioned upon works or worth.

God loves us in spite of our shortcomings.
Divine love is an attribute of God, for God is love.

The Apostle Paul enumerates the characteristics of God's divine love (I Cor. 13).

1. Divine love suffereth long: It can endure evil provocation without being filled with resentment or revenge. It will endure much with the one loved, and wait long to see the kindly effects of such patience.

2. Divine love is kind; It seeks to be useful; and not only seizes on opportunities of doing good, but searches them out.

3. Divine love envieth not: This love is not grieved at the good of others. Envy is the effect of a bad mind which is bent on ill will. The mind that is bent on doing good to all can never wish ill to anyone.

4. Divine love vaunteth not itself, is not puffed up. It does not have a false value of itself, therefore it is not bloated with self-conceit. It enables us to esteem our brethren, thereby limiting our esteem of ourselves. This love is not a boaster, it doesn't brag, talk big, does not raise tumult and disturbances. It calms the angry passions instead of raising them.

5. Divine love does not behave itself unseemly: It never does anything unbecoming to Christian morals or virtues, or that would bring reproach; but it behaves hospitably, with courtesy and good will toward all.

6. Divine love is an enemy of selfishness, seeketh not her own. It is true that self-love, in some degree is natural, but divine love cares for the neighbor as it does itself. It never seeks its own to the hurt of others, but will very often neglect its own for the sake of others.

7. Divine love is not exasperated; is not angered, irritated, provoked or annoyed. It is not easy for the flames of wrath to be kindled where the fire of love is burning. Anger has no lodging place in the bosom where love dwells. But anger will soon be resolved by concern.

8. Divine love thinks no evil; it cherishes no malice, nor does it give way to revenge. It is not suspecting of evil in others. Love covers faults that appear, rather than searching out those that are concealed.

9. Divine love rejoiceth not in iniquity. It wishes ill to no one, therefore it could never delight or rejoice in doing harm or mischief. It is compassionate for the sins of others, but receives no entertainment from them. Rejoicing in truth, love receives its satisfaction from seeing truth and justice prevail among men joined with a mutual faith and trust.

10. Divine love beareth all things. It is not blazing or publishing the faults of a brother or sister. Love will tell him or her in private in order that they will not be publicly exposed. It will always be patient upon provocation and long in patience in all things.

11. Divine love believeth all things, hopeth all things. It does not destroy prudence. This love will make the best of everything: Its judgments will always be sound, and its beliefs will be well. Should love be not able to believe well in others, it will always hope well.

Yes, the greatest thing in this world that shall last forever is love. As children of God it is only natural and supernatural for this type of love to be manifested in our lives. Our love should flow forth freely to all. God did not, nor does not, need a reason to love us, but quite the contrary. *"Christ died for us while we were yet sinners and that is God's own proof of His love toward us"* (Roman 5:8 NEB). God showed he loved us when we were in an unlovable condition by giving His Son to die for us, thereby redeeming us from the curse of the law and restoring us once again to the position of sons and daughters, with Christ. Jesus gave us a new commandment: *"Love one another; as I have loved you, so you are to love one another. If there is this love among you, then all will know that you are my disciples"* (John 13:34-35). He that loveth not knoweth not God, for God is love, and God is eternal.

Happy is the man that findeth wisdom, and the man that getteth understanding...She is a tree of life to those that lay hold on her.

By wisdom was the whole universe founded. It pours through it, hinges on it and is expressed in it. Her fruits are riches, honor, and length of days.

Those who desireth understanding to become the master of their life circumstances eat of the tree of life, which is in the midst of the paradise of God (Revelation 2:17).

Anyone that can understand, let him hear what the Spirit says unto the believer. You have a God-given right to be victorious in all your affairs.

Take ye eat

NETWORKING: WELL SPRINGS OF WISDOM

What is Networking? Very simply stated; it is keeping in touch with people you know, people of various backgrounds and occupations.

What is the benefit of networking? The answer is obvious; it is to have ready access to information and assistance when you are in need of such.

It is wise to know people of various backgrounds, and to have formed a warm relationship with them. If you have developed good relationships with those you meet, you will be able to call on them in the time of need. Seek out those whom you trust and respect, those with expertise in their field, then make it a point to get to know them. Keep in mind that to have a friend you must show yourself to be friendly. Be willing to give your assistance whenever opportunity presents itself. Never present yourself as being someone looking for a handout, you'll soon be recognized. But rather seek the opportunity to be of assistance, you will be awarded. Be careful whose friendship you seek! *"Make no friendship with an angry man; and with a furious man thou shalt not go"* (Proverbs 22:24). *"Be with wise men and become wise"* (Proverbs 13:20). Remember: *"A man's gift maketh room for him, and bringeth him before great men"* (Proverbs 18:16). *"Many favors are showered on those who please the* King"(Proverbs 16:15).

Networking is a system to be used to the good of all. Often you may be able to refer someone in need of a particular service to someone you personally know to be trustworthy. Both parties will be grateful and willing to offer you their assistance in return. The reasons for networking are numerous and you may want to think of some of the ways you can use the system for your benefit, and for the benefit of others.

How to begin your personal network:

1. First make a list of all the occupations and professions you can think of.

2. Inquire of others about people they may know in different professions.

3. Keep a list of names and noteworthy comments concerning them.

4. Be alert for opportunities for you to get to know them.

5. Make sure you present yourself in a favorable light, to be remembered.

6. Consider what favor you can do for them, then do it.

7. Finally, make a list of the ones with whom you have been able to form good relationships. Eliminate the less favorable or undesirable. Hold on to the good ones.

8. Stay in touch, don't allow them to forget you. But don't be a pest. Use every opportunity to keep your network working smoothly, to the good of all with whom you may have dealings.

"Through desire a man, having separated himself, seeketh and intermeddleth with all wisdom"(Proverbs 18:1).

Make a special effort for good relationships with;

A good doctor, a reputable attorney, a reliable mechanic, a sharp real estate broker, a prominent banker, and last but not least a well-informed God-fearing minister.

Keep a notebook of favors these people have done for you, and any kindness they may have shown. Make sure you express your appreciation appropriately. This may seem like a lot of trouble, but it pays off in great dividends!

If you follow these instructions, you're on your way to forming friendships more precious than rubies. *"Without counsel purposes are disappointed, but* in *the multitude of counselors they are established"* (Proverbs 15:22).

Your Network

Name: _____Occupation _____
Address _____City_____ State _____
Resident Phone _____ Business Phone _____ Zip _____
Comments: _____
_____
_____

Name: _____Occupation _____
Address _____City_____ State _____
Resident Phone _____ Business Phone _____ Zip _____
Comments: _____
_____
_____

Name: _____Occupation _____
Address _____City_____ State _____
Resident Phone _____ Business Phone _____ Zip _____
Comments: _____
_____
_____

Name: _____Occupation _____
Address _____City_____ State _____
Resident Phone _____ Business Phone _____ Zip _____
Comments: _____
_____
_____

Your Network

Name: _____Occupation _____

Address _____City_____ State _____

Resident Phone _____ Business Phone _____ Zip _____

Comments: _____

_____

_____

Name: _____Occupation _____

Address _____City_____ State _____

Resident Phone _____ Business Phone _____ Zip _____

Comments: _____

_____

_____

Name: _____Occupation _____

Address _____City_____ State _____

Resident Phone _____ Business Phone _____ Zip _____

Comments: _____

_____

_____

Name: _____Occupation _____

Address _____City_____ State _____

Resident Phone _____ Business Phone _____ Zip _____

Comments: _____

_____

_____

www.ingramcontent.com/pod-product-compliance
Lightning Source LLC
Chambersburg PA
CBHW060142050426

42448CB00010B/2250